IMAGES OF ENGLAND

Around
Droitwich

IMAGES OF ENGLAND

Around
Droitwich

Bob Field

NONSUCH

Cover picture: Land Army trainees at Hindlip Hall House farm in 1917.

First published 1997
This new pocket edition 2006
Images unchanged from first edition

Nonsuch Publishing Limited
The Mill, Brimscombe Port,
Stroud, Gloucestershire, GL5 2QG
www.nonsuch-publishing.com

Nonsuch Publishing Limited is an imprint of Tempus Publishing Group

British Library Cataloguing in Publication Data.
A catalogue record for this book is available from the British Library.

ISBN 1-84588-271-7

Typesetting and origination by Nonsuch Publishing Limited
Printed in Great Britain by Oaklands Book Services Limited

Contents

Acknowledgements

I would like to thank the following for permission to use their photographs in this book:

K.C. Adkins, Aerofilms Ltd, F.G. Ashmore, Mrs Badger, C.P. Bailey, J. Baker, R. Beach-Hicks, T. Bennett, *Berrow's Worcester Journal*, Rev L.J. Birch, *Birmingham Despatch & Mercury*, *Birmingham Post & Mail*, *Bromsgrove Messenger*, J.L. Brown, H. Buckle, G.J. Carder, R.V. Clarke, N.A. Clayton, E.H. Cockrane, J.A. Copson, J.K. Cornelius, R.F. Cotton, J.L. Davies, A.C. Derrick, A.W. Evans, H.C. Gadd, W.T. Gay, R. Goverlock, C.V. Hancock, L.E. Harper, Rev W.R. Hartley, Dr R.J. Hetherington, P. Hill, T. Hobson, W. Hodson, R. Hughes, C.J. Johnson, R.A. Jordan, S.J.B. Keaney, Brendan Kearney, G.F. Key, H.G. Kibblewhite, D. Kirkham, B. Lashbrook, A. Mapletoft, P.G. Matthews, P.R. Meller, A. Milne, R.H. Murray, E.J. Neild, A.F. Nicklin, F. Nichol, F.W. Pain, Miss E.A. Penn, L. Penn, P. Persake, W. Reid, C.R. Sayer, E.H. Sergeant, R.W. Sergeant, B. Sewell, E.W. Shallow, Ms M. Skinner, F. Smythe, Stockport Museum, Stoke Prior School, D.P. Verge, L.D. Watson, C.W. Webb, J.P. Weston, J. Whybrow, Miss M. Wight, S.A. Wood, A.S. Woodley, D. Wright, Mrs W.R. Young.

Introduction

Images and sound bites can be maligned, criticised and even mocked. We are often told that the present day is one which lacks a deep appreciation of standards, ethics, and scholarship. To publish a book of local photographs may – at cursory glance and without sound thought – appear to pander to modern tastes. And, indeed, it does, because any such book has to be attractive to its potential readers, while at the same time make at least a modest profit for both author and publisher.

This book does far more than that. However much is written, however much scholarship goes into a learned tome, nothing can replace the authenticity, the reality and the immediacy of the photograph. Photographs give a completeness of picture which the written word alone cannot hope to do. True, even photographs do not tell the whole story; they depend on light, angle, lens and the taker's sense of reality or creativity, or both. There is a world of difference between a simple shot of a village centre taken purely to record a street scene at any one particular instant, and the same scene taken for artistic purposes as, perhaps, autumnal shades of light and warmth stream across the image.

When the truth has been acknowledged, the skill, knowledge and personal inclinations of the author or compiler come into play. Even record photographs need explanation and interpretation. Books of local photographs such as this are subject to particularly careful, even intense, scrutiny by the many local people who make up their readership. Unless the author or compiler knows his or her craft inside out, mistakes will be made and judgements readily clouded.

It is particularly good to see a photographic compilation which does not relate to one particular town or city. More and more the distinctions between town, suburb and hinterland are blurred. Less and less are the agricultural, industrial and even social differences between rural and built-up areas to be identified. Social change is not approved of by all, but it has happened, happens now, and will continue to happen in the future. To have this published record of *Around Droitwich* is therefore, an important and interesting development in publishing and historical research and presentation.

The vast majority of originals of the photographs are held at the Worcester County Record Office, the fundamental source for local historian of the county. As years go by, the historians will not only use these 'traditional' written and photographic archive resources for research, but also newer digital media, film, video and oral sound recordings. It will be interesting to see how this develops. In the meantime this volume will provide an invaluable resource not only for local 'Droitwich' folk but for many miles around. It is a format which deserves to be emulated.

Life is short. We are who and what we are because of the environmental, family and social influence of the past, both before and during our actual lifetime. In turn, we are substantially responsible for shaping and influencing much of what happens in the future, both as individuals, and corporately, as part of the overall society in which we presently live.

Attractive, interesting, and appealing as it is, this book is also far more. It sets out, for a wide audience, images of what has helped shape them and the future to come.

Tony Wherry,
County Archivist, Hereford and Worcester County Council, 1996

The countryside around Droitwich includes a number of interesting villages and this compilation is intended to introduce you to some of them. They are all within seven miles of Droitwich and a circular route may be followed from Ombersley in the west, moving in a clockwise direction through Elmbridge, Stoke Prior, Dodderhill, Hanbury, Himbleton, Crowle, Tibberton and finishing with Salwarpe. It is not intended to be a history of the area - other books cover that - but there are a few historical references, particularly to the Gunpowder Plot in 1605 in which Worcestershire played an important part. Many of the photographs, which are all taken from the Worcestershire Photographic Archive at the County Record Office, have rarely been seen before.

Bob Field

One

Droitwich and Hadzor

Droitwich is a well-known town situated on the main Worcester/Bromsgrove road about halfway between the two towns. Its origins lie in an old salt-producing settlement with evidence of salt working in the Iron Age (800 BC to AD 43). The Romans built a fort here and there was also a large Roman villa in Bays Meadow. A charter was granted to the Borough of Droitwich by King John in 1215. The town still has many old buildings although some have been lost in rebuilding during the last thirty years. Droitwich was the centre of a network of 'salt-ways' leading north, south, east and west from the town and on these salt was carried to all parts of the country. Some of these 'salt-ways' ran along the old Roman roads. In 1768-71 a canal was built linking the town to the River Severn and this was used for the transport of salt and coal. The Droitwich Junction canal was built in 1854 linking this to the Worcester/Birmingham canal. The salt industry moved to Stoke Prior in 1892 (see Chapter 13) and the last salt works closed down in 1922.

   Hadzor lies on the eastern edge of Droitwich and the Worcester/Birmingham canal is on the east side of the village where it joins the Droitwich Junction canal. It is a small, scattered village with a deconsecrated church which contains monuments to the Amphlett and Galton families well known in the area in the eighteenth and nineteenth centuries. The manor was owned by the Amphlett family from 1633 and it passed to the Galton family in the nineteenth century. The main building now is a large office and conference centre.

Droitwich High Street in 1930 looking from the east.

Droitwich High Street in 1953.

The Star and Garter Inn, High Street, Droitwich in 1953. The earliest parts of this building date from the 1580s, some parts are from seventeenth century while the frontage was re-faced c. 1860, with some changes in the 1980s.

The Wagon & Horses Inn, High Street, Droitwich, 1962.

St Andrew's church and the Market Place in 1857. Parts of the church date from 1290. The tower was reduced in height in 1828 because subsidence caused by the brine streams had made it dangerous.

Droitwich Town Hall – built in 1826 opposite St Andrew's church – in 1957. It is now converted into commercial premises.

St Andrews Street, Droitwich in 1920, with the Raven Hotel (the original manor-house) on the right.

Above: The Old Cock Inn in Friar Street, 1920. It was licensed in 1712 during the reign of Queen Anne and it is said that Judge Jeffries held his Assizes there, although that has never been proved. The present building dates from the early nineteenth century.

Right: A close-up of the window of the Old Cock Inn, Friar Street. This window was originally in the old St Nicholas' church.

Priory House, Friar Street, 1950. This sixteenth-century building was refurbished in the seventeenth century and restored by the Droitwich Preservation Trust in the 1970s.

The Working Men's Club, Friar Street, Droitwich in 1953. This building, which dates from the nineteenth century, was formerly the local asylum run by Dr Ricketts, after whom the adjoining lane was named.

The old Saline Baths and Hotel, Droitwich featured on a print from 1857.

The later St Andrew's Brine Baths, built by John Corbett in 1887, photographed here in 1921.

The old Royal Brine Baths, 1953.

The interior of St Andrew's Brine Baths in 1953. The pool was very salty, there being 2.9 pounds of salt per gallon of water – saltier than the Dead Sea! It was not possible to sink, only float. There are now replacement brine baths in the private hospital complex on the same site.

Victoria Square, Droitwich in 1916, with the Raven Hotel at the rear and Salters Hall in the centre. The trees in front of Salters Hall have gone and the whole area is now paved.

Droitwich post office and the National Provincial Bank (now NatWest), 1953. The post office was built about 1905 in Victoria Square in the Baroque style

Lord Nuffield, the motor manufacturer and notable benefactor, being presented with the Freedom of the Borough in 1951. Dr Shirley Jones, a well-known local figure, was honoured at the same ceremony.

Salters Hall in Victoria Square was built in 1881 by John Corbett as a recreational place for his workers. It was demolished and replaced by a new building which became a cinema and which closed in 1963. Part of the building was then occupied by Midland Bank and Diana's Café. Many people will remember buying their ice-creams from Diana's Creamery! The building has since been converted into the public library.

The Worcestershire Hotel in 1905. This was one of the hotels built by John Corbett, 'the Salt King'.

A meeting of the Worcestershire Hunt outside the Worcestershire Hotel on Boxing Day, 1949. The hunt met there every year until the hotel was closed.

Droitwich policemen in 1887.

Part of the mosaics at the Sacred Heart Roman Catholic church on Worcester Road. The church was consecrated in 1932 and its walls are covered in glowing mosaics, said to be the best in Britain outside Westminster Cathedral. They are made of eight tons of tiny Venetian-glass squares.

Worcester Road, Droitwich, 1950.

Coventry Hospital (Almshouses), in the Holloway, 1953. They were built in the latter part of the seventeenth century as the result of a bet between Lord Coventry and Sir John Pakington. Additional buildings at the rear were added in 1902.

No 21 Queen Street, 1953. These are the remaining two bays of a late sixteenth-century timber-framed cottage, with added eighteenth/nineteenth-century door and windows. It is now an Indian restaurant.

Droitwich railway station, 1900. This shows the original building which was demolished in the mid-1980s.

The Great Western Railway Hotel, near the station, in 1953. It has since been demolished and the site is now occupied by light industry.

Hill End Cottage, Bromsgrove Road, 1953.

Manor House, St. Peter's, Droitwich

Above: St Peter's Manor, next to St Peter's church on the south-east side of Droitwich, 1908. The manor-house is dated 1618 but has been much modernised.

Left: An outsize belisha beacon on the Worcester Road, 1955. This was placed to warn motorists speeding down the hill into Droitwich.

Opposite above: An aerial view from the north-east of the centre of Droitwich, 1931. Dodderhill church can be seen on the right.

Opposite below: The centre of Droitwich from the north, 1931. The Worcestershire Hotel is in the centre with its gardens in front (now built on) and St Andrews Brine Baths on its right.

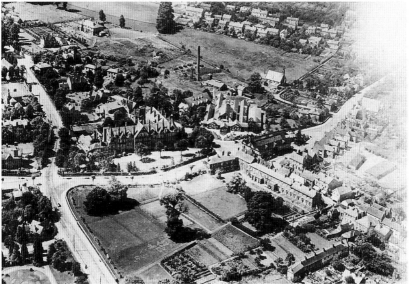

A view of Droitwich town centre from the north, 1931. The old Brine Baths chimney can be seen in the centre of the picture. Notice the amount of open space around the town at this time.

Droitwich seen from the north-east, 1931, with St George's Square in the centre and the Holloway running to the top left. The main Bromsgrove/Worcester road is on the right.

Above: A nineteenth-century print showing the village of Hadzor. It is a lithograph by W. Walton from a drawing by Mrs H. Galton.

Right: The church of St John the Baptist, Hadzor, which was restored in 1835 and 1866. There are parts dating from around 1300. The church has been deconsecrated and is now used as a storeroom.

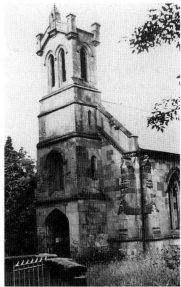

A round-house, near Hanbury Wharf in 1967.

The manor-house in Hadzor, 1971.

Two

Ombersley

This large parish (over 7,000 acres) is one of the most picturesque in Worcestershire, containing at least 28 listed buildings. It is situated on the conjunction of the Droitwich/ Tenbury and Stourport/Worcester roads (the latter now by-passing the village) some four miles west of Droitwich and includes Hawford and Hadley. It contains Ombersley Court, the home of the Sandys family who have been connected with the village since Edwin Sandys, Bishop of Worcester, bought the lease for the manor in 1560.

An eighteenth-century print of Ombersley Court. This has been the home of the Sandys family since it was built in 1724.

A print of St Andrew's church built 1825-29 and designed by the architect Rickman.

The Kings Head (now Kings Arms) and village in 1900. The public house was originally built about 1450 and is said to have been slept in by Charles II after the battle of Worcester.

Timbered houses in 1900.

A cottage at Horse Ferry in 1900.

The town mill, 1900.

Miller's house, 1900.

Main street with sheep in 1900.

The preaching cross in 1900. It has a fifteenth-century square base, the rest being seventeen or eighteenth-century.

Above: The Dower House, an early seventeenth-century two-storied half-timbered building, in 1900. This was the site of the old Court House which was in use until the Dissolution of the Monasteries in 1539.

Left: Hawford dovecote in 1948. The lower part was originally used as a coach house.

The main street in Ombersley, 1910.

A second view of the main street, from the opposite side, also taken in 1910.

Old houses in the village, 1914.

Village weigh-bridge, 1938.

Members of Hadley Green Bowling Club, 1906.

Hadley Green Bowling Club in 1937. Back row: A.O. Needham, G.H. Goddard, H. Gordon-Smith, H. Wheelock, T. Bates, S.S. Somers, R.J. Castley, H.R. Pullinger, E.M. Buck. Middle row: H.E. Tovey, John Stallard (cellarer and senior member), H.B. Worth (President), L.A.C. Southam. Front row: J.E. Rayer, H.S. Payne (chaplain), P.W. Robinson.

Cross Cottage, Hadley, a fifteenth-century cruck building.

The remains of the original Norman church of St Andrews in the present Ombersley church-yard.

Wyatt's antique shop, Hawford, in 1951.

A gipsy caravan which was set on fire in 1956 at Old Yardings farm following the death of its owner, Constance Annie Boswell, aged 27, the wife of Alfred Finney. All her possessions were included in the 'pyre' in accordance with an old gipsy custom. Over eighty Romanies were present.

Right: The village blacksmith, Mr Albert Clarke, in 1962, with a gate of his own design.

Below: Overbury Court, 1962.

Three

Doverdale, Hampton Lovett and Westwood Park

Just on the northern edge of Droitwich lie these three areas. Doverdale is on the road leading west from Hampton Lovett and is probably better known for its restaurant – the Ripperidge Inn. It is a very small parish – the population in 1901 was only 58 persons. The church has a timber and lead spire. Hampton Lovett manor was owned by the Pakington family from 1524 who built a house named Hampton Court. This was destroyed by Cromwell in the Civil War and the family then made their home in Westwood House. Sir John Pakington was a government minister in the nineteenth century and was MP for Droitwich. The manor passed out of the family in 1900. Westwood Park was part of Dodderhill parish until 1178, then annexed to Hampton Lovett in 1541 but still extra-parochial until 1857. It is south of Hampton Lovett and lies just north of the Droitwich/Ombersley road, surrounded by a stone wall. The house was built on the site of a nunnery with the surrounding park, established by the Pakingtons in 1618, being stocked with deer. The house is now converted into flats.

Church of St Mary in Doverdale, restored in 1860, but with fifteenth-century glass in one north window.

There are many old features in the church of St Mary, Hampton Lovett which was restored in 1858-9. One of the earliest parts is the fourteenth-century south-porch tower. Rumour has it that Oliver Cromwell rested his horses here during the battle of Worcester. This photograph was taken *c.* 1900.

A nineteenth-century engraving of the ground plan of Westwood House and Park.

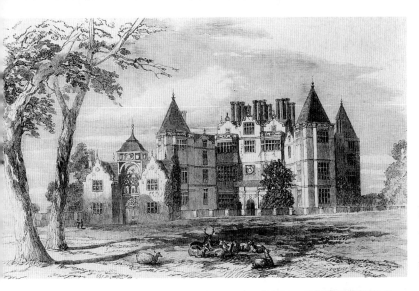

Above: The front of Westwood House in 1852. This is built on the site of a Benedictine nunnery. After the dissolution of religious houses, the land passed to Sir John Pakington who built the house in the reign of Queen Elizabeth I as a lodge or banqueting house.

Right: The front porch of Westwood House, 1900.

The entrance to Westwood House in 1899, photographed from the hall steps.

The saloon at Westwood House, 1900.

Four

Rushock, Elmley Lovett and Elmbridge

North of Droitwich are these three small agricultural villages. Rushock was a chapelry of nearby Chaddesley Corbett and is off the Droitwich/Kidderminster road. It is well wooded, being originally part of the Feckenham and Ombersley forests. Rushock was the home of the noted Royalists, Henry Townshend and Francis Finch. Elmley Lovett and Elmbridge are south of Rushock, the latter once being a chapelry annexed to Dodderhill. It eventually became a separate parish in 1877 and includes the Purshall estate.

The vicarage, Rushock, 1958.

St Michael's church, Rushock, originally constructed in 1258 and rebuilt in 1758.

Church of St Michael, Elmley Lovett, 1905. This was rebuilt in 1839-40, but the fourteenth-century west tower was retained.

Above: The Forester's Club, Elmley Lovett, in 1916. The back row includes William Serrell (5th from left) and George Serrell (8th) and the front row includes Alfred Chance (1st) and Jim Sprage (2nd). On the extreme right is John Cliton of the Live and Let Live Inn.

Right: A dovecote in the old rectory garden at Elmley Lovett, built in the seventeenth century.

Church of St Mary, Elmbridge, rebuilt in 1872, but still including parts dating from *c.* 1190 to 1200.

Road making at Elmbridge in 1924 using 'Roller No. 15 Aveling' and 'Porter No 10318/1922'.

Five

Upton Warren

This village is situated three miles from Droitwich on the Bromsgrove road, just north of Wychbold. Upton Warren is a small village but the area attracts a lot of visitors due to the presence of Webbs Garden Centre, and to a lesser extent, a nature reserve run by the Worcestershire Nature Conservation Trust, and a sailing centre on the site of the old gravel pits. One of the notable houses in the parish is Badge Court which originally belonged to the Wintour family (see Huddington Court, Chapter 9) and later to the Talbots.

St Michael's church and thatched cottage. The church is mainly fourteenth-century although there are earlier features.

Left: The dovecote at Badge Court, 1900.

Below: Badge Court in 1952. This half-timbered and brick house was built *c.* 1630 and was originally the home of the Earl of Shrewsbury.

Webbs seed-trial grounds as they were in 1952. The site is now a garden centre, one of the largest in the country, and recently recognised by a sign on the M5 motorway.

The Swan Inn in 1956. This is a former coaching inn with in its heyday twenty coaches on the Birmingham/Worcester route calling there each day. It has now been extended to include a Travel Lodge.

An aerial view of Upton Warren village taken in 1956. The light-coloured patch of ground at the bottom of the picture is the site of gravel extraction workings. Their excavations gave rise to a theory that Upton Warren was largely a swamp and water-hole area to which prehistoric animals came. Remains of mammoth, woolly rhinoceros, bison, reindeer and wild horses have been found. The 'Swan Inn' can be seen at the junction of the lane and the main road (A38).

Rev Harold Goddard – the flute-playing vicar of Stoke Prior, Wychbold and Upton Warren – in 1978. A flute was once used instead of the organ at St Michael's church, Upton Warren. This centuries-old tradition went out of fashion in the 1930s. The flute was presented to the diocese by Mrs Mary Willet and was once played by her great-grandfather, Mr Thomas Hyde.

Six

Stoke Prior

This village, originally a hunting lodge frequented by King John, is four miles north-east of Droitwich on the Bromsgrove/Alcester road and in the valley of the River Salwarpe. It grew much larger after salt extraction commenced there in 1828 and it became the home of John Corbett's Salt Works, which eventually closed in 1972. It is situated on the Worcester/Birmingham canal which was used for the carrying of salt in large quantities. It is also on the main Birmingham/Bristol railway line with its own station named Stoke Works.

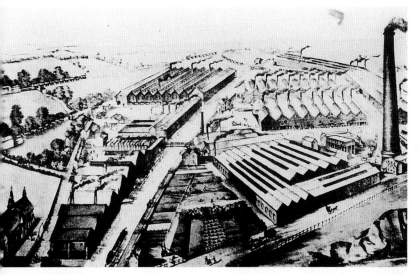

An 1876 lithograph of the salt-works.

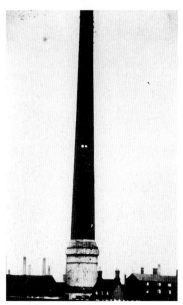

Left: The main chimney for dispersing chemical fumes in 1890. It was approximately 300 ft high – the third highest in the country – but was reduced by 95 ft in 1930.

Below: The road from Finstall to Stoke Prior in 1889. It is now filled in.

The back of The Pools in 1899.

Astwood Court, 1899.

Cutting hay in 1899.

The Bowling Club, 1904.

The Dockyard in 1906. It opened in 1883 and closed in 1933 and was originally owned by the Farrin Brothers. Mr George Farrin is shown standing on the deck of the first motor-driven boat (*Enterprise*) built in the dockyard. Also in the background (second from left) is Mr Thomas Farrin and his father is in the centre of the picture.

Cut-lump salt wrapping girls, 1920.

Sagebury Terrace in 1907.

Sagebury Terrace in 1962.

Stoke United Football Club, 1907.

Railway bridge No 90 on the LMS (London, Midland and Scottish) Railway, pictured from the south in 1910.

A class at the National School in 1908.

A Council School class in 1910.

A photograph of the Council school in 1915.

Death and Dividend Society committee, 1916.

A Bible class in 1916.

The violin class with the Headmaster, Mr T.C. Williams, and the Misses Lambie (teachers).

An outing from a public house in 1920.

A D-Day celebration parade in 1944.

Stoke Works station, 1950.

Hampstalls barge, 1951.

Foley Gardens, 1951.

St Michael's church, 1952. The building dates back to the late twelfth century.

Left: The village post office, 1954.

Below: The brine reservoir and a view of the salt-works in 1954.

Seven

Dodderhill

This area (there is no village of Dodderhill) includes Wychbold, a separate ecclesiastical parish since 1888, and the hamlet of Rashwood. It lies on the Worcester/Birmingham road just north of, and adjoining, Droitwich. Another part, In-Liberties, which borders the Junction Canal, was transferred to Droitwich in 1884. Wychbold was a royal residence for the kings of Mercia in the ninth century although the site of that building is not known. The largest, and best known, building is the Chateau Impney, which was built in 1875 by John Corbett and modelled on a French chateau. Corbett built many cottages in the district for the salt workers employed at his Stoke Prior Salt Works (see Chapter 6). Another large building was Wychbold Hall, the property of Judge Amphlett, which in 1936 was demolished due to subsidence, as was the replacement house in the late 1950s. Wychbold is the site of another local landmark – two 700-ft high masts at the BBC transmitting station.

Dodderhill church (St Augustine's). A prominent landmark on a hill overlooking Droitwich, the church here was originally built in the late twelfth century and was consecrated in 1220.

Left: Dodderhill Common in 1898.

Below: Wychbold village post office in 1900.

The Robin Hood Inn, Rashwood, as it was in 1930.

The south lodge at Château Impney.

The Chateau Impney. This was built by John Corbett for his wife.

An interior view of the Chateau Impney, showing the hall and staircase as it was in 1950.

Plaque on a house in Crown Lane, Wychbold, marking the nineteenth century home of the Archbishop of Canterbury.

The Church of St Mary, Wychbold, the building of which in 1888-9 was financed by John Corbett 'the Salt King'.

The Wychbold paper mill in 1974.

Miss Rose Adelaide Heeley on her 111th birthday at Rashwood Nursing Home in 1975. She was then believed to be Britain's oldest resident.

Eight

Stock and Bradley, Hanbury and Bentley Pauncefoot

Stock and Bradley, including Stock Green and Bradley Green are west of Feckenham on the Droitwich/Alcester road. It is a well-wooded area, formerly part of Fladbury. Hanbury is a large hilly parish east of Droitwich on the Droitwich/Alcester road with the Bromsgrove road leading north from the centre of the village. The church is situated high on a hill just outside the village and adjoining Dodderhill Common (known locally as Hanbury Woods). The village has been associated with The Archers radio programme (as have several other Worcestershire villages!). Hanbury includes the hamlet of Broughton Green which contains Mere Hall, an imposing old timber-framed building and the original home of the Bearcroft family. The other notable old houses are Hanbury Hall, with its fine landscaped gardens, previously the home of the Vernon family, and Broughton Court. Bentley Pauncefoot was an old manor held before the Norman Conquest by Leofric. It was originally part of Tardebigge. The name Pauncefoot is an old family name, Richard Pauncefoot holding land at Bentley in 1198.

St John the Baptist church, Bradley, 1952. It was built in 1864-65.

The Baptist chapel in 1935. In the gateway are Olive and John Dimond. John was later organist at the chapel.

Stock Green Baptist chapel in 1976.

Above: Middle Beanhall farm, a timber-framed sixteenth-century building with brick star chimney stacks.

Right: A charities board in Bradley church.

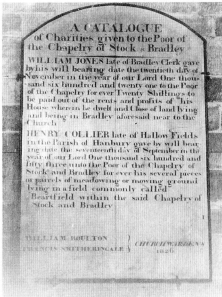

A CATALOGUE
of Charities given to the Poor of
the Chapelry of Stock & Bradley

WILLIAM JONES late of Bradley Clerk gave by his will bearing date the twentieth day of November in the year of our Lord One thousand six hundred and twenty one to the Poor of the Chapelry for ever Twenty Shillings to be paid out of the rents and profits of his House wherein he dwelt and Close of land lying and being in Bradley aforesaid near to the Church

HENRY COLLIER late of Hallow Fields in the Parish of Hanbury gave by will bearing date the seventeenth day of September in the year of our Lord One thousand six hundred and fifty three unto the Poor of the Chapelry of Stock and Bradley for ever his several pieces or parcels of meadowing or mowing ground lying in a field commonly called Beartfield within the said Chapelry of Stock and Bradley

WILLIAM BOULTON
FRANCIS SMITHERINGALE } CHURCHWARDENS 1826

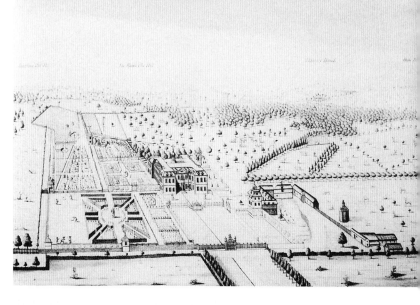

A 1720 print of Hanbury Hall and park. This was completed in 1701 for Thomas Vernon, whose family had bought the manor in 1631. It was the residence of the Vernon family for many years but is now a National Trust property.

A nineteenth-century print of Hanbury Hall, a Queen Anne brick house with stone dressing.

Above: An early photograph of Hanbury Hall, *c.* 1900.

Right: Sir George Vernon at an auction of his family treasures outside Hanbury Hall in 1935.

Broughton Court, a fifteenth-century timber-framed and whitened brick building with eighteenth-century additions, 1899.

The smithy at Hanbury in 1900.

The front of Mere Hall in 1907, showing the entrance gates. This was once the home of the Bearcroft family.

Mr Edward Coles, wheelwright, of Mere Green, 1952, with a gate made from brougham wheels.

Above: The Moorlands, Hanbury, in 1950. A half-timbered house, built *c.* 1619 and extended in 1879, it was once used as an almshouse.

Left: The eighteenth-century colombarium at Pump House farm, Mere Green.

Opposite above: Bishops Hall farm in 1950, which was eventually used as an outbuilding.

Opposite below: St Mary's church, Hanbury is a well-known local landmark, as it is situated high on a hill outside the village. Earliest parts of the church date from around 1210.

Pipers Hill Common notice from 1959.

Mr Hanlet Russell of Hanbury, glass engraver, in 1962.

Cross and Hands Cottage, Hanbury, believed to be a fifteenth-century building, pictured here in 1959.

Well Cottage, Pumphouse Lane, Hanbury.

IN MEMORY OF THE MEN OF HAMPTON
WHO DIED FOR THEIR COUNTRY

IN THE

1914		1919
L.T.M. PARKER	GEORGE	H.M.'S SIMPSON
A.B.S. SMITH	CECIL FRANK	R. NAVAL DIV.
PTE. BALLARD	JOHN	WORC. REGT.
PTE. BARLEY	HUBERT	R. ENGINEERS
PTE. BAYLIS	REGINALD	WILTS. REGT.
L.CPL. BRAZIER	EDWARD JOHN	WORC. REGT.
PTE. BRAZIER	HENRY	WORC. REGT.
L.CPL. BRAZIER	WALTER	STAFFS. REGT.
PTE. BRAZIER	WILLIAM HENRY	STAFFS. REGT.
PTE. CALLAWAY	CHARLES THOMAS	WORC. REGT.
PTE. DIXON	WILLIAM	WORC. REGT.
PTE. GOWER	DAVID	CANADIAN INF.
PTE. HALL	CHARLES HARRY	S.W. BORDERERS
PTE. HICKLIN	JOHN EDWARD	WARWICK REGT.
PTE. NORWOOD	HERBERT THOMAS	WORC. REGT.
PTE. PASS	JAMES	GLOS. REGT.
PTE. POLLARD	ALFRED	WORC. REGT.
PTE. PUGH	WILLIAM HENRY	R. FUSILIERS
PTE. SHEPPARD	HENRY	WORC. REGT.
PTE. SHEPPARD	JOHN	ARMY'S CORPS
PTE. SMALL	JAMES	WORC. REGT.
PTE. SMITH	HARRY	WORC. REGT.
PTE. SMITH	FRANK LEONARD	WARWICK REGT.
PTE. STANTON	ALFRED WILLIAM	WORC. REGT.
PTE. TURNER	HARRY	GRENADIER G.
PTE. WEAVER	FREDERICK	WORC. REGT.
PTE. WENSLEY	ERNEST	WORC. REGT.
PTE. WRIGHT	HARRY	WORC. REGT.

THEY LOVED NOT THEIR LIVES UNTO THE DEATH. REV.12:11.

Left: Memorial in St Mary's church to those who perished in the First World War (1914-18).

Below: Mr Albert Reeves, master thatcher, scything reeds to be used to rethatch a cottage in Crowle, 1983.

St Mark's chapel, Salt Way, Hanbury.

Bentley Manor was built on the site of a watch-tower in Feckenham Forest and dates back to the sixteenth century. During the Second World War it housed the 267th Field Battery, Royal Artillery, then the Essex Regiment, the Royal Engineers and US troops, after which it was used as a prisoner of war camp and then for displaced European nationals. Pictured here in 1930, it was demolished in 1950.

Tardebigge farmhouse at Lower Bentley (1967) is a listed building, believed to be 400 years old. There is a legend that at one time it was a small convent. Built in two sections, it was of a type known as a large hall house. For many years it was the home of the Leadham family, and was then called Webb House.

Nine

Huddington and Himbleton

Huddington is five miles south-east of Droitwich and includes the hamlet of Sale Green, one mile north-west of the village. Its main building is the sixteenth-century timber-framed Huddington Court, famous for its connection with the Gunpowder Plot. It was here that the conspiracy was hatched – Robert Catesby, the chief plotter, being the cousin of Robert and Thomas Wintour who lived there. When the plot was discovered on 6 November 1605, the brothers fled to Huddington Court. However, they were soon captured and were executed in December 1605. It is said that the ghost of Robert still roams the house with his head tucked under his arm! Glass from Huddington church can be seen in the Raven Hotel, Droitwich.

Himbleton, four miles south-east of Droitwich, and seven miles north-east of Worcester, includes the hamlets of Shell, Shernal Green, Phepson, Earls Common and Dunhampstead (although part of the latter is now in Oddingley). The village has many half-timbered houses dating from the sixteenth and seventeenth centuries and the church was originally built in a clearing in Feckenham Forest.

Church of St James, Huddington, standing very close to Huddington Court. The earliest remaining feature is a window dating from c. 1300.

HERBY WHEN DIGGING THE GRAVE OF KETURA
DAVIDSON IN 1903, WERE FOUND THE REMAINS OF A
UNKNOWN MAN WHO, FROM THE FACT THAT WIT
HIM WERE SCOTS COINS OF KING JAMES VI AND KIN
CHARLES I AND A FRENCH COIN OF LOUIS XIII,
DOUBLE TURNOIS DATED 1637, IS BELIEVED T
HAVE BEEN A FUGITIVE FROM THE ROYAL ARM
DEFEATED AT WORCESTER ON 3rd SEPT 165

A gravestone in Huddington churchyard relating to the Civil War.

Huddington Court, a fifteenth-century half-timbered house, originally home of the Wintour family associated with the Gunpowder Plot.

A half-timbered cottage at Huddington, 1938.

The dovecote at Huddington Court, 1938.

Above: Fox Inn, Sale Green about to close in 1959 as it was without running water or adequate sanitary facilities.

Left: A cider press at Court farm, Huddington, 1969.

Opposite: The church tower of St Mary Magdalene, Himbleton.

Above: Church of St Mary Magdalene, Himbleton, 1970. This was originally built in the twelfth century and was enlarged in the thirteenth and fourteenth centuries.

Left: Dovecote at the manor-house, Himbleton, 1952. The manor was formerly the residence of Sir Douglas Galton KCB.

Shell Manor, a sixteenth-century half-timbered building with nineteenth-century brick additions, pictured here in 1952.

Galton Arms, Himbleton, originally named The Harrow (or Arrow), then the Douglas Galton Arms. It has changed little since 1953.

Court farm, a late sixteenth-century half-timbered building. Himbleton church can be seen in the background.

Himbleton House, also known as Brook House with Bow Brook running to the rear.

Shell Cottage in 1963 before its restoration.

View of Saleway farm and its lily pond.

Himbleton Manor, 1896.

Galton's House, 1954.

Ten

Churchill, Broughton Hackett and Crowle

These three villages are about five miles south-east of Droitwich. Churchill is a small village containing a few farm houses and half-timbered cottages. Broughton Hackett, situated on the Worcester/Alcester road, is also small and is mainly pasture land. Crowle is a larger, and very old village. It has a Saxon charter dating from the ninth century and is also mentioned in the Domesday Book. One of the village's main buildings was Crowle Court but this was destroyed in 1864. However, most of the moat can still be seen as can the tithe barn and what is believed to be the kitchen block in its grounds.

Churchill Mill in 1976, mention of which is made in the Domesday Book. It has been extensively restored by the owners although some of the millstones and a nineteenth-century waterwheel have been retained.

An interior view of Churchill Mill.

The church of St Michael, Churchill was heavily restored in 1910, but the south doorway and chancel arch are thirteenth/fourteenth-century.

St Leonard's, Broughton Hackett, considered the oldest church in Worcestershire. The nave is probably twelfth-century and the chancel thirteenth-century.

Two dovecotes, with the one at Morgan's farm, Broughton Hackett, pictured on the left in 1900. It collapsed in the late 1950s. Right: the dovecote near Church House, Broughton Hackett, 1936.

Toll-house, Broughton Hackett, 1954.

Cider mill, Broughton Hackett, 1974.

Above: Hop kilns, Broughton Hackett, 1974.

Right: Mr J.L. Read, Broughton Hackett PCC secretary, examines the 400-year-old churchwarden's seat, 1974.

Left: Fourteenth-century timber church porch at Crowle with an original roof, photographed in 1920.

Below: Two portraits of Crowle men. Left: shepherd Ernest Pugh, pictured in 1952, aged 69. He worked for the Wythes family at Rectory farm, Crowle, for over fifty years. His father served the same family for 45 years. Right: the woodcarver and historian, Harry Wythes, by this time a 'retired' farmer and a churchwarden at Crowle for 45 years, pictured in 1959.

Tithe barn, Crowle, 1955. It is now under threat of demolition.

Church of St John the Baptist, Crowle, with a sixteenth-century tower arch. The church was rebuilt in 1881-85.

Fireplace in the main room of one of the Malthouse Cottages.

Malthouse Cottages, Crowle, photographed in 1957 before their restoration.

Eleven

Tibberton and Oddingley

Tibberton is five miles north-east of Worcester and four miles west of Droitwich. The Birmingham/Worcester canal runs along the northern boundary. It is a quiet village off the main roads. Oddingley is about three miles south-east of Droitwich and is best known for the 'Oddingley Murders' in the last century. A dispute about the payment of tithes had arisen between the local farmers and the Rector, Rev George Parker, who was shot in 1806. The alleged assassin, Thomas Hemming of Droitwich, disappeared, but his body was found in 1830 at Netherton farm with a fractured skull. Three suspects were tried but all were acquitted.

The Plough, Tibberton, as it was in 1899. This is where the plotting for the Oddingley murder took place in 1806.

Left: Mrs Salisbury of Tibberton working on a glovers 'donkey' in 1932.

Below: The village toll-house at Tibberton road junction, 1953.

Right: The village smithy, Tibberton, 1954.

Below: Rectory farm, situated near Tibberton church, in 1954.

The beagles of the Wyre Forest Hunt being exercised by huntsmen Lawton Evans and W.A. Catterby at Moat farm, Tibberton, 1959.

The late fifteenth-century church of St James, Oddingley was restored in 1851. In 1806, the Rector, Rev George Parker, was shot and bludgeoned to death following a dispute over tithes.

A dovecote with Oddingley church in the background, 1906.

Rose Cottage, Oddingley, 1955.

Mr Sutton of Oddingley, making an ornamental garden figure in 1955.

Twelve

Bredicot, Spetchley and White Ladies Aston

These three villages lie about three to four miles east of Worcester just off the Worcester/ Alcester road. Bredicot is a tiny village bisected by a railway line. It has a picturesque group of sixteenth and seventeenth-century houses, mostly half-timbered and brick. The manor was granted to the church of Worcester before the eleventh century. Spetchley was the home of the Berkeley family for over 500 years. It has large formal gardens (30 acres) laid out in the seventeenth century, and a deer park with red and fallow deer, all open to the public. The manor also belonged to the church of Worcester before the ninth century and part of it was granted to the monks of Worcester in 988 AD. White Ladies Aston is another small village which adjoins Spetchley. The name comes from the colour of the habits of the Cistercian nuns who owned the manor, which was part of the manor of Northwick at the time of the Domesday Survey (1087). The village had strong connections with the White Ladies nunnery at Whistones, Worcester, which was founded in the thirteenth century.

Bredicot village main street in 1954.

Above: The rear view of Bredicot Court in 1954. This is an early seventeenth-century half-timbered and brick house with eighteenth-century additions.

Left: Late thirteenth-century church of St James in Bredicot. The building was heavily restored in 1843.

Spetchley Park, home of the Berkeley family for over 500 years, pictured here in 1951.

The village smithy, Spetchley, in 1961.

All Saints' church, Spetchley. Parts of the building date from *c.* 1300, but it now no longer used as a church.

Owls End Cottages, White Ladies Aston, 1951.

An 1890 engraving of the church in White Ladies Aston, including a plan and some interior detail.

Church of St John the Baptist, White Ladies Aston, pictured in 1932. Most of the building dates from the early 1860s although there are some Norman features.

Left: Aston Court farm, White Ladies Aston, with its unusual chimney, 1951.

Below: Church Cottages, White Ladies Aston, 1951.

Thirteen

Salwarpe, Martin Hussingtree and Hindlip

These three villages, now combined under a single rector, are south of Droitwich, each lying off the Worcester road. Salwarpe lies to the west of the main road, the old village being in a cul-de-sac just beyond the Droitwich/Worcester canal which runs by the church. Next to this is Salwarpe Court, an old building connected with the Beauchamp family, Earls of Warwick, and then with the Talbots. Martin Hussingtree is bisected by the main road, the main part lying to the west. This parish was formed by the manors of Hussingtree (listed in the Domesday Book) and Martin. The land at one time was held by Westminster Abbey. Martin Court farm was once the home of the Jacobean organist and composer, Thomas Tomkins, who is buried in the churchyard. Hindlip lies to the east of the main road. It was a chapelry of St Helen's, Worcester at the end of the eleventh century. The parish also includes Smite, transferred from Warndon in 1880, being mainly farms. The largest building in Hindlip is Hindlip Hall on the site of the original Hindlip House, which was a refuge for Roman Catholic priests in the late sixteenth century. It was occupied by Thomas Habbington, whose sister married Thomas Winter, famously associated with the Gunpowder Plot. The hall, built in the 1820s, is now the headquarters of the West Mercia Police.

St Michael's church, Salwarpe, with features dating from c. 1200 and a fifteenth-century tower.

Left: The road to Salwarpe Court in 1930.

Below: Porters Mill House in 1936. Originally built in 1066, it was restored in 1503.

Salwarpe Rectory in 1951, now converted into flats.

Salwarpe Court, a sixteenth-century building, and reputed to be the birthplace of 'Warwick the Kingmaker'. The house was later endowed to Catherine of Aragon when she married Prince Arthur.

Above: Middleton Cottage, Salwarpe.

Left: Brookhill Cottage, Ladywood, Salwarpe.

The Old School House, Salwarpe, now used by a video company.

Salwarpe Mill in 1969, mentioned in the Domesday Book, but now demolished.

The hub of Salwarpe village in 1979. Church Cottage, originally a school, is on the left. The lychgate is on the right.

Oddcroft, formerly a mission hall, in Pulley Lane, Salwarpe.

St Michael's church, Martin Hussingtree, the earliest parts of which date from c. 1200.

Martin Court farm, 1953. Formerly the manor-house, this building dates from the eighteenth century.

Mr Bert Wynne as Santa Claus in 1955, pictured outside a thatched cottage in Martin Hussingtree, with Leslie Higgins, Gerald Dennchy, Mrs J. Baldwin, David Baldwin, Alan Dennchy and Sally Sharp.

Brookhill Cottage, Ladywood, Salwarpe, 1956.

The Swan Inn, Martin Hussingtree, photographed in 1960. It has recently been extended.

A 1776 print showing the south-east view of Hindlip House.

St James' church, Hindlip. This was almost entirely rebuilt in 1864, although it retains some fourteenth and fifteenth-century features.

Land Army trainees at Hindlip Hall House farm in 1917.

Shell Cottage as it was in 1955 with visitors admiring part of an unusual garden at 'Harvey Dene', Smite Hill, which took the owner, Sidney Dowdeswell, and his wife Elsie, over 50 years to complete. Miniature statues, a castle, concrete arches, fountains and mosaic work in shells, porcelain and glass were all to be found among the flower beds. Friends and relatives who had holidayed in this country or abroad provided the shells, and the coloured glass and porcelain came from a variety of sources such as broken china, beer bottles, etc. People from all over the world visited the garden and it was featured in many guide books and overseas magazines. Mr Dowdeswell worked as inspiration struck him, creating no regular pattern but adding, at his whim, goldfish, flowers, penguins, peacocks, butterflies or fishermen. Many visitors commented that 'it must be a full-time job', but it was not. Mr Dowdeswell worked all his life in a factory at Worcester and claimed to have cycled 40,000 miles on his way to and from work. His garden was his hobby. There was no charge for admission – only a charity box. Mr Dowdeswell died in 1977 at the age of 93 and his wife, unfortunately, was unable to continue his work. The house was sold and the garden sadly broken up in 1980.

Left: The early seventeenth-century dovecote at Lower Smite farm.

Below: The late sixteenth-century timber-framed former Hindlip Rectory, 1979.